AXIS PARE

A PARENT'S GUIDE TO YOUTUBE

A PARENT'S GUIDE TO

YOUTUBE

axis

Tyndale House Publishers
Carol Stream, Illinois

Visit Tyndale online at tyndale.com.

Visit Axis online at axis.org.

Tyndale and Tyndale's quill logo are registered trademarks of Tyndale House Ministries.

A Parent's Guide to YouTube

Designed by Lindsey Bergsma

For information about special discounts for bulk purchases, please contact Tyndale House Publishers at csresponse@tyndale.com, or call 1-855-277-9400.

Library of Congress Cataloging-in-Publication Data

A catalog record for this book is available from the Library of Congress.

ISBN 978-1-4964-6730-0

Printed in the United States of America

28	27	26	25	24	23	22
7	6	5	4	3	2	1

YouTube is the new TV.

JOHN LYNCH, *BUSINESS INSIDER*

CONTENTS

A LETTER FROM AXIS

Dear Reader,

We're Axis, and since 2007, we've been creating resources to help connect parents, teens, and Jesus in a disconnected world. We're a group of gospel-minded researchers, speakers, and content creators, and we're excited to bring you the best of what we've learned about making meaningful connections with the teens in your life.

This parent's guide is designed to help start a conversation. Our goal is to give you enough knowledge that you're able to ask your teen informed questions about their world. For each guide, we spend weeks reading, researching, and interviewing parents and teens in order to distill everything you need to know about the topic at hand. We encourage you to read the whole thing and then to use the questions we include to get the conversation going with your teen—and then to follow the conversation wherever it leads.

As Douglas Stone, Bruce Patton, and Sheila Heen point out in their book *Difficult Conversations*, "Changes in attitudes and behavior rarely come about because of arguments, facts, and attempts to persuade. How often do *you* change your values and beliefs—or whom you love or what you want in life—based on something someone tells you? And how likely are you to do so when the person who is trying to change you doesn't seem fully aware of the reasons you see things differently in the first place?"[1] For whatever reason, when we believe that others are trying to understand *our* point of view, our defenses usually go down, and we're more willing to listen to *their* point of view. The rising generation is no exception.

So we encourage you to ask questions, to listen, and then to share your heart with your teen. As we often say at Axis, discipleship happens where conversation happens.

Sincerely,
Your friends at Axis

---

[1] Douglas Stone, Bruce Patton, and Sheila Heen, *Difficult Conversations: How to Discuss What Matters Most*, rev. ed. (New York: Penguin Books, 2010), 137.

IT'S NOT JUST FOR WATCHING SILLY VIDEOS NOW AND THEN. GEN Z "CAN'T LIVE WITHOUT" YOUTUBE.[1]

EVER HEARD OF MRBEAST'S real life *Squid Game* challenge?[2] Seen random celebrities eat really spicy wings?[3] What about this YouTuber named Jake Paul who keeps getting all the headlines with his boxing career?[4]

These are all what we might call "cultural events" that occurred on or because of YouTube, a social video sharing platform. At over 2 billion, the number of YouTube users is second only to those on Facebook (2.9 billion monthly)[5], and YouTube receives more than 122 million visitors per day.[6] To look at it another way, people around the globe are collectively watching more than a billion hours of content on YouTube each day.[7]

The days when you used to wait till Saturday night to watch your favorite show are long gone. This might be old news to you—after all, Netflix has grown pretty popular. But when asked which online service they couldn't "live without," 67% of users ages 13–24 named YouTube, with 85% saying it was something they regularly watch.[8] YouTube easily surpassed Netflix, traditional TV, and other social media platforms such as Facebook and Instagram. So what's the appeal? What are they watching that they can't live without? What are all the different subscriptions now associated with the platform? How do we talk to them about it all? And most importantly, how do we teach our children to set healthy boundaries around *all* of their media usage, including YouTube?

How do we teach our children to set healthy boundaries around *all* of their media usage, including YouTube?

WHAT IS
YOUTUBE?

SIMPLY PUT, YOUTUBE is a social media platform for sharing videos with people. Users can limit themselves to watching, liking, and commenting on other people's videos, or they can create channels and post their own videos. Former PayPal employees Jawed Karim, Steve Chen, and Chad Hurley created YouTube in 2005.[9] This infographic[10] shows some of the major highlights of YouTube's history up through 2012. Now a multibillion-dollar company owned by Google, people use YouTube for just about anything you could imagine and for many purposes you would never think of. It's almost difficult to conceive of the internet without it.

WHAT CAN YOU WATCH ON YOUTUBE?

THE LIST IS SO LONG, it's rather difficult to answer this question. You can see your favorite movie clip, replay the latest Super Bowl halftime show, or watch some guy named PewDiePie freak out while he plays video games. You can watch celebrities compete with Jimmy Fallon, discover how to fix something around your house, or giggle at adorable animals. Whether it's music videos, interviews with your favorite athletes, or news updates, you can find almost anything you want to see on YouTube.

YouTube is unique in: 1. its breadth and variety of content; and 2. how it has democratized who can gain fame and influence. One friend of ours believes that YouTube is the "most underrated influential platform of the day." You just have to compare the audiences of a popular TV series and a well-known YouTuber's videos to see the truth of that statement. The season 4 finale of *Yellowstone* at the end of 2021 drew just over 9 million viewers.[11] For comparison, it's not uncommon for individual MrBeast videos to rack up 25+ million views in their first week.[12]

YouTube is unique in:
1. its breadth and variety
of content; and 2. how it
has democratized who can
gain fame and influence.

HOW DOES IT WORK?

WATCHING VIDEOS ON YOUTUBE is pretty straight-forward. Simply go to the website, search for what you want to find, and click on whichever videos you'd like to view. When watching videos, you can expect to encounter ads and/or annotations, which are essentially pop-ups that people can add at various points in their videos. Whenever a YouTube video ends, another will start playing automatically. If you click Cancel to stop the next video from autoplaying, you'll see a grid of related videos you might be interested in watching next.

Anyone can watch videos on YouTube, but you have to sign in with your Google account if you want to comment on, like, or share them. Signing in allows you to post your own videos as well.

You can also create playlists of your favorite videos and subscribe to other users' YouTube channels. In addition to your desktop computer, YouTube can be accessed through the mobile app or your smart TV.

WHAT'S YOUTUBE PREMIUM?

YOUTUBE PREMIUM is a subscription YouTube offers.[13] Basically, users can watch ad-free videos, as well as original TV shows with YouTube stars, even when not connected to the internet. The subscription also includes access to YouTube Music and the ability to listen to videos with one's screen turned off.[14] It starts at $11.99/month, after a three-month free trial.

There's some confusion over what YouTube Premium is supposed to be: a platform similar to Netflix or Hulu, or one more like Spotify?[15] Either way, for Gen Z, if their favorite YouTube stars are in a YouTube Premium show, they will want a subscription.

WHAT'S YOUTUBE TV?

AN ALTERNATIVE to cable television (billing itself "cable-free live TV"), YouTube TV[16] offers many of the shows and networks previously only available through traditional cable or satellite subscriptions (including NFL, NBA, and MLB networks), as well as all YouTube Premium original shows. It costs $64.99/month and is now available on various smart TV devices, in addition to portable and handheld ones.[17] It also offers the ability to record shows to a cloud-based DVR that has no storage limits.

Since its launch in 2017, YouTube TV has expanded to include more networks, providing the majority of Americans with access to local and cable networks on their devices. As it has already done with its main platform, YouTube is continuing to reinvent "the television experience for the new generation."[18]

WHAT'S YOUTUBE KIDS?

AS YOU MIGHT GUESS, YouTube developed YouTube Kids[19] (YT Kids) for the purpose of giving kids a safer YouTube experience, since people can post whatever they want on YouTube (until they get reported or flagged). And because millions of people are on YouTube, it's not difficult to run across something inappropriate.

YT Kids purports to be a "world of learning and fun, made just for kids" and a "safer online experience."[20] The app does have a lot of kid-friendly content on it: shows like *Winnie the Pooh*, kids' songs, and educational material.[21] Parents can create a profile with videos tailored for their kids and even set a limit on how long their kids can be on the app. YT Kids has parental controls that enable parents to prevent their children from searching for videos on their own. However, there is no way to block content in advance of encountering it. You have to block inappropriate videos as they come up.

And inappropriate videos do come up on YT Kids. Certain people in the world like to create content that seems kid-friendly—so YouTube's algorithm doesn't flag it as inappropriate—that turns out to be disturbing. On the YT Kids home page, YouTube even admits that its system isn't perfect and that inappropriate videos do make it through. Common Sense Media strongly recommends that you do not allow your children to search for videos on their own on YouTube Kids. They also recommend that you supervise closely and watch videos with your kids as much as possible if you choose to let them use the app. We briefly looked into the app and noted that one of the shows featured heroines that were pretty sexualized.

In 2017, YouTube came under criticism for inappropriate videos on YT Kids.[22] But disturbing content is still appearing there,[23] with YouTube admitting that it needs to do more. If you'd rather go with a service that has tighter parental controls and closer oversight, check out the apps at commonsensemedia.org/app-lists.

There is no way to block content in advance of encountering it. You have to block inappropriate videos as they come up.

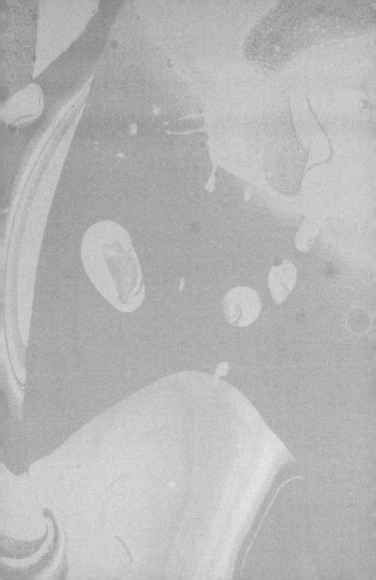

WHY DO KIDS (AND YOUNG ADULTS) LIKE YOUTUBE?

AS A PARENT, it's easy to feel as though YouTube is just another app for you to worry about. It might seem like the only purpose of the platform is for your kids to waste time watching pointless videos. So what's good about it, and why do teenagers like it so much?

IT'S EASY TO CONSUME, EDUCATIONAL, AND ENTERTAINING.

One reason younger people like YouTube is that it's easy to consume. It only takes a few seconds to access, it's visual, and the videos don't require a huge time commitment since they are often only a few minutes long.

In addition, because the videos on it are free to watch (thanks, ads!), YouTube has given us much easier access to a wide range of educational content, much of which is excellent.

As we've already said, YouTube is a new form of entertainment. It's one of the main ways modern young people like to relax and unwind. See Common Sense Media's video "What Kids Are Watching on YouTube" to get a general idea of some of the most popular types of videos that teens enjoy watching.[24] If you enjoy watching a show or a sports game on TV to relax, that's really not that different from how kids are using YouTube. It's just a different platform and format.

IT'S ON DEMAND.

Unlike broadcast TV, YouTube videos are always there, available whenever a person wants to watch them. Viewers aren't required to be available at a prescribed time to see content, which offers a certain amount of control: *I* can watch what and when *I* want to for as long as *I* want. This kind of control was unprecedented

The biggest current cultural moments of our society, even if they don't originally air on YouTube, will make it there quickly.

before YouTube. Platforms like Netflix, Prime Video, and Hulu now offer similar control, but YouTube still has the edge in terms of sheer hours of content available and types of content.

IT'S CULTURAL AGGREGATION.

One of the biggest appeals of YouTube is that it's one of the main places where culture is "happening." If you want to know the latest news in pop culture and society at large, there are plenty of YouTubers who will collect the highlights and give commentary on them.

The biggest current cultural moments of our society, even if they don't originally air on YouTube, will make it there quickly. These include presidential speeches, Super Bowl interviews, Olympic triumphs, and genuinely heroic moments, such as when pilot "Sully" Sullenberger safely landed a plane in the Hudson River.[25] YouTube is a convenient platform for staying abreast of the events of the day.

IT'S RELATABLE AND AUTHENTIC.

Because YouTube is a social media platform, it has provided opportunities for people to have a voice who never would have had one before. YouTube has made it much easier for the average person to gain a following and become famous.

The rising generation values authenticity and relationships. One result of these characteristics is that teenagers tend to trust the stars they follow on YouTube more than they trust traditional celebrities, partially because they feel that YouTube stars are more relatable.[26] Mainstream celebrities carefully craft an image or even keep their personal lives

YouTube stars not
only seem more relatable
but often do engage with
their fans more than the
average celebrity does.

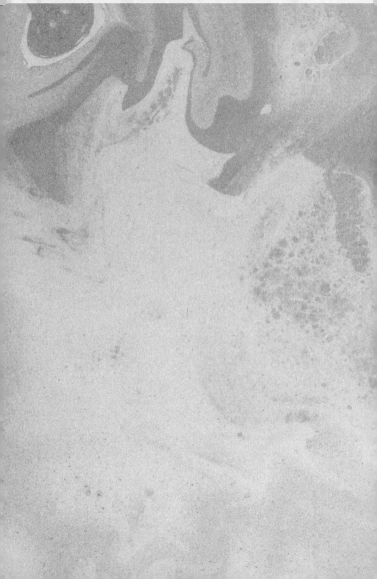

hidden, but people who have made it on YouTube generally seem more authentic (whether or not they actually are) because they are more open and often willing to show more of their everyday lives. It's easy for teens to see YouTubers as their peers.

YouTube stars not only seem more relatable but often do engage with their fans more than the average celebrity does. And somewhat ironically, because viewers value YouTube so highly, YouTubers who respond to culture often become influencers of culture themselves, so users want to pay attention to them for that reason as well.

WHAT ARE THE DANGERS OF YOUTUBE?

WASTING TIME

It's not uncommon for people to remark that they went on YouTube to watch one video and then got sucked into watching videos for hours on end. One eighteen-year-old girl we spoke to said she never got enough sleep and, when asked why, explained that it was because she had to be on YouTube making sure she didn't miss anything. She usually did this until 2 or 3 a.m. every night, regardless of whether she had school the next day.

YouTube is in fact *designed* for this to happen. That's why another video automatically starts loading when the one you're watching is finished (though the Autoplay feature can be turned off[27]).

Beyond doing what you can to protect your kids from objectionable content, make sure you're teaching them what good stewardship looks like. How can you help them develop good habits when it comes to how much time they spend on YouTube? How will they know when they've gotten too much of a good thing and it has become a bad thing?

COMMENTS

Reading through the comments on YouTube is like studying the graffitied bathroom stalls of the internet. These comments almost always contain statements that are explicit, obscene, and offensive. Or, if they aren't vulgar, they're usually garbage. Allowing your children to read the comments will almost certainly expose them to graphic content, so we recommend enabling Restricted Mode in order to turn them off. See page 61 in this booklet for how to do so.

EXPLICIT CONTENT

One easy way to encounter inappropriate content on YouTube is in the advertisements that run before a video. It's also possible for the suggested videos that appear after a video ends to be inappropriate. Some users like to "troll" by posting a video that looks safe but then cuts to something objectionable right in the middle of it.

As with many other social media apps, because there is so much content on YouTube, the platform largely relies on users to police what gets uploaded.[28] Whenever a system is run in this manner, mature content *always* gets through, so there's a chance that kids will be exposed to it. The website Defend Young Minds notes that YouTube actually tolerates explicit content, particularly if those posts are earning a lot of money.[29] More on that next.

PERVERTED CONTENT THAT SEEMS KID-FRIENDLY

It's very important not to assume that YouTube channels that look kid-friendly *are* kid-friendly. Some channels that appear to be clearly intended for kids have bizarre, violent, or sexual content in them.[30] These videos range from being a bit strange to being perverse. In 2017, several videos featuring Spider-Man and Elsa[31] as characters included content that was fairly weird (the content was sometimes called "Elsagate"[32]). Other videos showed cartoon characters like Mickey and Minnie Mouse acting out various types of deviant and twisted behavior. Videos like these are often published on channels with words like *toys* or *family* in them so they seem safe.

Although it contains strong language throughout, H3H3 had a conversation with Post Malone about Elsagate[33] which

Reading through the comments on YouTube is like studying the graffitied bathroom stalls of the internet.

does give a pretty good analysis of how content like this can be targeted to kids through YouTube's algorithms. After the controversy over these videos, many of them were removed, and YouTube started relying more heavily on algorithms to remove explicit or harmful content more quickly.[34] This means that now many more videos are being removed than before. However, as Aleks Meiusi points out, the moderation system is still imperfect, and there will always be things that slip through.[35]

It *is* possible to use YouTube and never run across content like this. We're not trying to scare you into never letting your kids use YouTube again. But we do want to give you fair warning of the dangers on the platform and emphasize the importance of you, the parent, vetting the content your children are watching.

WHAT SHOULD I DO?

HISTORICALLY SPEAKING, Christians have struggled with how to react to changes in culture. While it takes work, we recommend teaching your kids how to use YouTube wisely. Doing so will be more helpful than going to one extreme of banning it completely or the other extreme of letting them watch whatever they want. Obviously, when and how you decide to let your kids use YouTube will depend on how old they are and your assessment of their maturity. Here are some suggestions for steps to take in that regard.

PARENTAL CONTROLS

If you opt to download YouTube Kids, don't allow your kids to search for videos on their own. Curate the videos for them, watching them ahead of time or at least watching them with your children.

As far as YouTube itself goes, parental controls are helpful to a point. If you use Restricted Mode, it will hide the comments for you. To turn on Restricted Mode, go to the YouTube menu and click on Settings. At the very bottom of the screen, you'll see the option to turn the Restricted Mode on or off.

Note that Restricted Mode will catch some of the worst content out there, such as excessive violence or nudity, but it will not catch all inappropriate content, as we mentioned earlier. Also, you might have Restricted Mode turned on for one browser, but someone could still use YouTube with Restricted Mode turned off by using a different browser, a private browsing tab, or a different account. Frankly, the only way you can be *absolutely* sure that your kids are not being exposed to mature content is by either watching videos before they do or by watching videos with them.

However, you can implement a few other strategies to have more oversight of what your kids are watching. You can turn off Autoplay so that when one video is done, another doesn't immediately start playing. This will help prevent an inappropriate video from automatically starting. To turn Autoplay off, start playing any YouTube video. Then click on the gear icon at the bottom of the video. You'll see an option to toggle Autoplay on or off.

Another strategy is to subscribe to channels you know you're okay with your kids watching. You could also create playlists for them with videos you've already watched. Finally, you could add a third-party filter.

SORRY, REVIEWS WON'T HELP THAT MUCH.

It would be great if someone could rate and review every YouTube channel that existed, but reviewing channels is possible only at a minimal level. Influence4you .com has a list of the top 10 most subscribed YouTubers at the time of this writing (remember—these will likely change before too long).[36] You can also go to the website Social Blade for detailed metrics on the most popular YouTube channels, videos, and genres.

But the amount of content on YouTube is so extensive and diverse that your children almost certainly watch many other videos and channels besides the most well-known ones. It's simply not practical for people to evaluate YouTube channels in the same way they could write a movie review. Not only is the amount of content on YouTube enormous, but it

Make sure your
children know that
if they see a video
that disturbs or scares
them, they can come
to you and you won't
be angry with them.

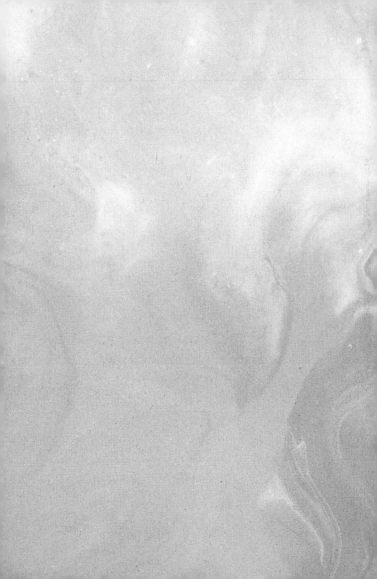

also changes quickly. Even if you rated a popular influencer such as PewDiePie one year, he could reinvent himself the next year,[37] and your review would be obsolete.

WE NEED TO TALK TO OUR KIDS, NO MATTER HOW OLD THEY ARE.

While we're not going to have advanced conversations with our younger children about what they're watching, we think it's critical to prepare them for encountering inappropriate content online. **This is true even if we're doing everything we can think of to protect them from it.**

Think about how you would have a conversation to protect your kids in case they encounter a sexual predator. You wouldn't go into great detail, but you'd make sure they understand no one should say certain things to them or ask certain things of them. If anyone ever does, they should come to you immediately and not be afraid to tell you what happened.

Use a similar strategy when it comes to your kids' online experience, even if you are tightly controlling their internet use. Make sure your children know that if they see a video that disturbs or scares them, they can come to you and you won't be angry with them. If they hear words they don't understand, they should ask you what they mean. If they see someone's private parts, they should tell you and not be afraid. Having a conversation like this won't hurt anything, and you could end up protecting them in an unexpected situation.

It's essential they know that they can talk to you without fear. Countless people are accidentally exposed to online porn at young ages. They then develop addictions to it because they were curious and/or afraid to tell their parents. It's no longer a question of *if* you need to have these conversations with your kids. You need to have them, *with your girls as well as your boys*. Assume they will be exposed, and do everything you can to prepare them for that possibility.

WHAT ABOUT TEENS?

A good rule of thumb is: **Don't rely on anything in and of itself to filter out inappropriate content.** There is simply too much content for a third-party service to screen out everything that would be bad for your children to see.

Another rule of thumb that applies to all your kids on some level is: **Be aware of what videos your children are watching.** With your younger kids, you'll have more control over what they watch. With your older kids, you should try to be aware of what they're viewing and give them guidance. Try asking your older kids the following questions to get a sense of their online activity:

- What's trending today?

- What channels do you subscribe to?

- What's in your library?

- What was the last video you shared?

ENGAGE WITH WHAT THEY LOVE.

Can you remember being a kid and loving something that your parents didn't understand or care about at all, like collecting baseball cards or playing Pac-Man at the arcade? How much would it have meant (or did it mean) to you to have your parents really try to understand

It's no longer a question of *if* you need to have these conversations with your kids. You need to have them, *with your girls as well as your boys*.

why you loved the music you did or what you enjoyed so much about your favorite hobby? In the same way, if your kids love a certain YouTuber or have a favorite video, ask them to tell you about it. Take the time to care and to understand why they like it. Even if the content is silly or immature, they will appreciate you making an effort to understand their world.

Here are some questions about YouTube you can discuss with your children:

- What do you like about YouTube?

- What do most of your friends like to watch on YouTube?

- What are some of your favorite videos on YouTube? Favorite channels? Favorite YouTubers?

- Have you learned new things on YouTube?

- How do you think people are using YouTube in good ways?

- How have you seen people using YouTube in bad ways?

- Have you ever run across inappropriate content? What did you do?

- What if you started watching a video you thought you'd enjoy, but realized it contained disturbing, graphic, or otherwise inappropriate content? Would you click away, or would you keep watching it?

- How can you tell when a video is bad enough that you need to click away? What makes it hard to stop watching a video once you've started?

If your kids love a certain YouTuber or have a favorite video, ask them to tell you about it. Take the time to care and to understand why they like it.

- How can you tell when it's a bad idea to watch a video in the first place?

- What are some of the consequences of viewing graphic content?

- What's an example of a YouTube video that you think took something too far?

- What's a reasonable amount of time to spend on YouTube?

- How can you guard against letting YouTube consume your free time?

- How can your time on YouTube enhance your time off YouTube?

DISCIPLE THEM IN HEALTHY HABITS.

We recommend coming up with a contract with your teenagers for how they use their phones. Even if you don't want to be so formal with how you structure their time on YouTube, it's still good to make your expectations clear. Your kids should know what they should and shouldn't watch and what the consequences of breaking those rules will be.

Encourage healthy family habits overall when it comes to technology. **We recommend having a policy not to allow devices in bedrooms at night.** This rule will help you and your kids rest better (since you won't be staring at a screen for hours before going to bed). And it will make it easier for your kids not to watch porn or other inappropriate content in private. You could also put limits on how much time they spend on the internet.

As always, pray, pray, pray. It's so easy to forget about the importance of prayer, and it can feel like we're not doing much when we do pray. But prayer is the most powerful and effective resource we have at our disposal. Pray that God would bring anything that your teenagers are hiding from you into the light. Pray for protection from the enemy. Pray for their hearts to be wholeheartedly devoted to the Lord. Pray for them to hate what God hates and love what He loves. Pray for them to use their time wisely.

Encourage healthy family habits overall when it comes to technology. We recommend having a policy not to allow devices in bedrooms at night.

CONCLUSION

DESPITE ITS DANGERS, YouTube is a good resource that can be used prudently. Filters and parental controls are helpful, but they're not a one-stop solution. You must remember that supposedly kid-friendly content on YouTube is not always safe, and you must guide your children on how to use the platform well.

The most important point to remember is that God is ultimately and finally in control. When your kids push your boundaries and watch content they know they shouldn't, He will be faithful. He will provide the wisdom you need as you seek it from Him. Remember, He loves your kids even more than you do.

ADDITIONAL RESOURCES

1. "Parents' Ultimate Guide to YouTube," Common Sense Media, https://www.commonsensemedia.org/articles/parents-ultimate-guide-to-youtube

2. "Parents' Ultimate Guide to YouTube Kids," Common Sense Media, https://www.commonsensemedia.org/articles/parents-ultimate-guide-to-youtube-kids

3. "Yes, You Can Make Six Figures as a YouTube Star . . . and Still End Up Poor," *Business Insider*, https://www.businessinsider.com/how-much-money-youtube-stars-actually-make-2014-2

4. "Can YouTube Survive the Adpocalypse?" *New York Magazine*: https://nymag.com/intelligencer/2017/12/can-youtube-survive-the-adpocalypse.html

5. "Deep Neural Networks for YouTube Recommendations," https://research
.google/pubs/pub45530/

6. Check out axis.org for more resources, including *The Culture Translator*, a free weekly email that offers biblical insight on all things teen-related

NOTES

1. Emma Bazilian, "Infographic: 50% of Gen Z 'Can't Live without YouTube' and Other Stats That Will Make You Feel Old," Adweek, May 21, 2017, https://www.adweek.com /performance-marketing/infographic-50 -of-gen-z-cant-live-without-youtube-and -other-stats-that-will-make-you-feel-old/.

2. "$456,000 Squid Game in Real Life!" YouTube, video, 25:41, November 24, 2021, https:// www.youtube.com/watch?v=0e3GPea1Tyg.

3. "Tom Holland Calls for a Doctor while Eating Spicy Wings | Hot Ones," YouTube, video, 27:35, December 9, 2021, https://www .youtube.com/watch?v=qxGmGGmvFD8.

4. "Jake Paul Scores Insane KO of Tyron Woodley in Round 6 | SHOWTIME PPV," YouTube, video, 2:50, December 18, 2021, https://www.youtube.com/watch?v =1xzYLkxjdag.

5. Brian Dean, "How Many People Use YouTube in 2022? [New Data]," Backlinko, updated September 7, 2021, https://backlinko.com /youtube-users.

6. Dean, "How Many People Use YouTube in 2022?"

7. Dean, "How Many People Use YouTube in 2022?"

8. Todd Spangler, "Younger Viewers Watch 2.5 Times More Internet Video than TV (Study)," *Variety*, March 29, 2016, https://variety.com /2016/digital/news/millennial-gen-z-youtube -netflix-video-social-tv-study-1201740829/.

9. Joe Watson, "When Was YouTube Created and Why (3 Key Reasons)," Watson Post, June 24, 2021, https://www.watsonpost.com/when -was-youtube-created-and-why/.

10. amazinjosh, "A Brief History of YouTube [Infographic]," Shortymedia, accessed March 14, 2022, http://www.shortymedia .co.uk/a-brief-history-of-youtube -infographic/.

11. Mason Bissada, "'Yellowstone' Season Finale Reaches 'Game of Thrones'–Level Ratings—Here's How It Stacks Up against Other Historic Shows," *Forbes*, January 5, 2022, https://www.forbes.com/sites/masonbissada/2022/01/05/yellowstone-season-finale-reaches-game-of-thrones-level-ratings-heres-how-it-stacks-up-against-other-historic-shows/?sh=7bd70a9b3ea3.

12. "MrBeast," Social Blade, accessed March 14, 2022, https://socialblade.com/youtube/user/mrbeast6000.

13. "YouTube Premium," YouTube, accessed March 14, 2022, https://www.youtube.com/premium?app=desktop.

14. "YouTube Music," YouTube, accessed March 14, 2022, https://music.youtube.com/tasteprofile.

15. Sahil Patel, "Neither Hulu nor Netflix nor Spotify, YouTube Red Is Having an Identity Crisis," Digiday, February 14, 2018, https://digiday.com/future-of-tv/neither-hulu-netflix-spotify-youtube-red-identity-crisis/.

16. "YouTube TV," YouTube, accessed March 14, 2022, https://tv.youtube.com/welcome/.

17. Bill Frost, "YouTube TV Review 2022: Plans, Cost, and More," ed. Mikayla Rivera, CableTV .com, December 10, 2021, https://www .cabletv.com/youtube-tv.

18. Joan E. Solsman, "YouTube TV: Millennials Will Love TV on Their Phones, Trust Us!," CNET (April 5, 2017), https://www.cnet.com /tech/services-and-software/youtube-tv mobile-phone-streaming-millennials/.

19. "YouTube Kids," YouTube, https://www .youtube.com/kids/.

20. "YouTube Kids," YouTube.

21. Caroline Knorr, "Is YouTube Kids Actually Safe for Kids?," *HuffPost*, November 14, 2017, https://www.huffpost.com/entry/is-youtube -kids-actually-safe-for-kids_b_5a0b50c5e4b0 60fb7e59d44b.

22. "Elsagate," Wikipedia, https://en.wikipedia.org /wiki/Elsagate.

23. Aleks Meiusi, "These Kids Channels Are Still Horrifying, Here's Why," YouTube, video, 25:24, September 23, 2021, https://www.youtube.com/watch?app=desktop&v=lDgWkZeEZo4.

24. Caroline Knorr, "What Kids Are Really Watching on YouTube," Common Sense Media, March 15, 2016, https://www.commonsensemedia.org/articles/what-kids-are-really-watching-on-youtube.

25. "NTSB Crash Animation US Airways 1549 w/ CVR and Audio Hudson," YouTube, video, 4:33, June 11, 2009, https://www.youtube.com/watch?app=desktop&v=5S5hRRio-E8.

26. Andrew Arnold, "Why YouTube Stars Influence Millennials More than Traditional Celebrities," *Forbes*, June 20, 2017, https://www.forbes.com/sites/under30network/2017/06/20/why-youtube-stars-influence-millennials-more-than-traditional-celebrities/.

27. "Autoplay Videos," YouTube Help, accessed March 14, 2022, https://support.google.com/youtube/answer/6327615?co=GENIE.Platform%3DAndroid&hl=en.

28. Kristen A. Jenson, "Keep Kids Safe: 9 Ways Porn and Predators Will Target Kids in 2018," Defend Young Minds, January 11, 2018, https://www.defendyoungminds.com/post /keep-kids-safe-porn-predators-target-kids -2018.

29. Jenson, "Keep Kids Safe."

30. Brian Koerber, "Gaming the System," Mashable, accessed March 14, 2022, https:// mashable.com/feature/youtube-kids-app -violent-videos-seo-keywords#6LzoSSzTfaq0.

31. "Spider-Man and Elsa Videos," Know Your Meme, accessed March 14, 2022, https://know yourmeme.com/memes/spider-man-and-elsa -videos.

32. "Elsagate," Wikipedia.

33. "Post Malone and H3H3 Try to Make Sense of 'Elsagate,'" YouTube, November 18, 2017, https://www.youtube.com/watch?app=deskto p&v=geJ5l331Hfo.

34. Kim Lyons, "YouTube Took Down More Videos than Ever Last Quarter as It Relied More on Non-Human Moderators," The Verge, August 25, 2020, https://www.theverge.com/2020 /8/25/21401435/youtube-videos-moderators -filters-human-appeals.

35. "These Kids Channels Are Still Horrifying, Here's Why," YouTube.

36. Shruti Hedau, "The Most Popular YouTubers of 2022," Influence 4You, November 29, 2021, https://blogen.influence4you.com/the-most -popular-youtubers-of-2022/.

37. Ben Popper, "Can PewDiePie Grow Up without Alienating His Fans?" The Verge, February 10, 2016, https://www.theverge.com /2016/2/10/10958434/scare-pew-die-pie -youtube-red-original.

PARENT'S GUIDES
BY AXIS

It's common to feel lost in your teen's world. These pocket-sized guides are packed with clear explanations of teen culture to equip you to have open conversations with your teen, one tough topic at a time. Look for more parent's guides coming soon!

BUNDLE THESE 5 BOOKS AND SAVE